My Life, My Story

My Life, My Story

Bonnie J. Lewis

I dedicate this book to my precious daughter,
Janine. God bless her.

CONTENTS

My Childhood

I was born on July 25, 1941, in Ponca City, Oklahoma, to Archie and Maye Fancher Young. I was a preemie, weighing in at a whopping three pounds. My first crib was a shoe box in my parents' bedroom. They kept me real close, that way they could keep an eye on me. I eventually graduated up to a dresser drawer.

When my dad married my mom, he already had seven children from a previous marriage. Together they added three girls and one boy, me being the youngest girl. Dad's first set of kids were already teenagers by the time I was born, so I don't really remember much about them from that time, as they all grew up, graduated, and moved out. Mostly, it was us last four kids. I did get to know my older brothers and sisters, though, when they would come back to visit, or when we would go visit them.

My dad was the night superintendent at Ponca City Continental Oil Company. When he retired, he had a poultry farm on a tract of land up the road from our house.

My mom was a stay-at-home mom. I don't know how she managed to cook for eleven kids. She was busy all the time. In fact, she had a nervous breakdown from all the work she did.

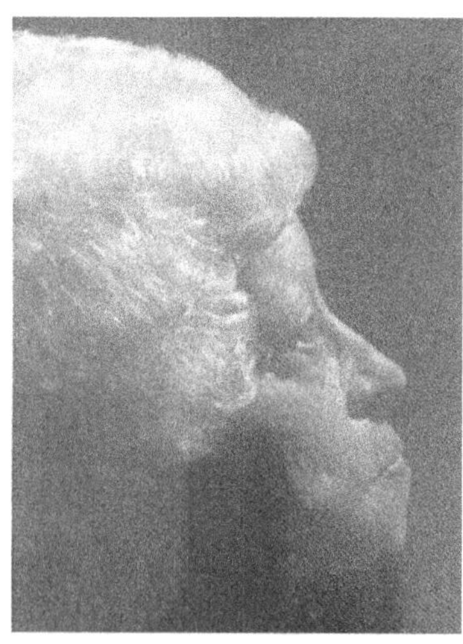

My dad put her in Coyncamble Hospital. The doctor there told him that she needed to get out more, so the kids were elected to clean the house. Mom worked in a large garden outside, and she loved it. Dad also saw to it that she went to all the ballgames with him, and that helped her quite a bit.

My dad was a deacon in the First Baptist Church of Ponca City. I remember how much I enjoyed church as a child. I went every Sunday. My favorite person in the church was Mildred Perry, she was head of the W.M.U. (Women's Missionary Union). After I grew up, I would go visit her and stay for a weekend or so. She was so much fun.

My School Years

In kindergarten, my favorite things to do were play and take naps.

In first through sixth grade, I enjoyed making friends, learning to print (cursive later on), and arithmetic.

I was very shy in junior high school, but I did have one special friend that I ran around with. We shared the same first name and we both joined the band.

In high school, I had many outstanding memories. My good friend, Bonnie, and I both joined the band again, which was called the "Big Blue." We learned to march to the yard line and make formations at the football games. Our school took first place in the band competitions ten years in a row.

In my senior year, we were invited to march in the Rose Bowl Parade in Los Angeles. We sold candy bars and other things to help pay for the trip. We took two big buses (it was a big band) and sang "99 Bottles of Beer" the whole way. We stayed in a big hotel. In the parade, we marched behind Paladine and his horse. We had to watch where we stepped! I made a lot of wonderful memories on that trip.

I loved English and enjoyed creative writing. My teacher, Mrs. Oates, always gave me A's on my stories. She said I was good, and I enjoyed it so much. At one time I aspired to be a teacher, but I changed my mind later when I was awarded a scholarship to nurse's training. It was for $325.00. Big money in 1959.

My Nursing Career

I took my first pre-entrance test in Muskogee, Oklahoma, but I was scared and didn't make it. I then went to Enid, Oklahoma, and tried again, and I passed. Our hospital there was called Enid General Hospital. It was a diploma school, and we had professors and nurses for teachers. We were called pre-clinical first-year students.

They assigned upper classmen as "big sisters." They sometimes gave us a hard time, but it was all in good fun. They would short sheet our beds and put small pebbles and sand in them. Sometimes they would stretch cellophane over the toilets (It was clear and you couldn't see it. Use your imagination!).

After six months of training, we were put in charge of the floors. Talk about scared. We had a very nice instructor, though, named Clara Brentlinger. She said if we had any questions we could call her. I'll admit, I called her all the time. She never minded, though. We also learned a lot from the older students.

After we worked the floors, we were then put in charge of the hospital from three o'clock until eleven at night. I came out of my shyness then, because when you're the boss, everybody comes to you with questions and complaints. I always had to talk to the doctors, patients, and staff. It was hard but fun, especially as time went on and I started getting more confidence. I loved my patients and looked forward to seeing them. Making rounds with the doctors was fun, too.

The last year of training, they farmed us out for six months to other schools for training in O.B. and psychiatry. They called us affiliates when we went to other schools.

I had trouble with O.B. in Tulsa. We had an instructor named Ms. Smith. She would walk constantly around the room, very intimidating, and then she would stop abruptly and put her face right in front of my face. She scared me to death. To make a long story short, I'll just say she flunked me out of school. I was crushed and went home in a deep depression.

I got a call from the director of the school, who wanted me to come back. She said they would send me to St. Anthony's Hospital for my training. I was so happy. I had thought my career was over.

I went to St. Anthony's Hospital and took OB-GYN classes. It was a snap course. It was the second time around and I made A's.

I then affiliated to St. Louis, Missouri, for my psychiatry training. There were two thousand students there. It was very interesting, and I really enjoyed it and learned a lot.

Then came graduation and time for state boards. It was a hard test, but I did fine and passed with flying colors. My highest score was in psychiatry.

A stipulation to my scholarship was that I had to work in a Baptist Hospital for a year. I stayed in Enid and worked out my year.

The outstanding part of my life was my nursing career. For the first time in my life I felt important, needed, and wanted.

I remember I had a little elderly lady who had cancer of the brain. They operated on her. Her husband was so devoted. He was at her bedside most of the time. She died and he was just beside himself. I took him to a room where the nurses gave reports on the patients. I gave him some coffee and called his daughter for him. I told her he needed someone with him, so she came up to the hospital. I was so sad for him. Months and months later, they had a beautiful plant delivered to me at the hospital. I almost cried I was so touched.

I believe that my nursing career kept me going and kept me from going to the psychiatric hospital myself, as a patient.

The Air Force

I then decided to join the Air Force. It sounded fun and glamorous. My first assignment for basic training was in Montgomery, Alabama.

I had never driven out of the state before, never even used a map, so that was interesting. I drove all day, and as it was getting dark, I decided to stop at a Holiday Inn for the night. I had a nice meal and went to bed happy.

I started early the next day, got directions, and drove all day long till nightfall again. I ended up at the *same* Holiday Inn that I had left that morning!

I didn't realize it at the time, but I was considered AWOL. I finally arrived at my post the next day. No disciplinary action was taken, because I had called and told them I had car trouble. A lie, I know, but I just couldn't tell them the truth.

My experience with the Air Force was just that, an experience I will never forget. I had planned to make a career of it, but things don't always work out the way you think they will.

I had a woman major, Major C, who just about ruined my life. She was on my back constantly. I couldn't please her, no matter what I did. No one could stand her. She was particularly hard on all the nurses, but she seemed to single me out. I felt like I was her number one whipping post.

One time, she told me she wanted me to take the BP (blood pressure) and TPR (temperature, pulse, and respiration) of all the troops in the ward. There were thirty to forty patients, so it took me a while. When I was done, I gave my list to her. She said it was wrong and that I had to do it all over again. I was so embarrassed. The troops were all so nice about it, though. Then, when I was about to go off duty, she called me back and told me my shoes needed to be polished.

One day, we had a bad snowstorm and I got stuck in it. I was late for work. She had a fit, just went on and on. You would have thought it was a federal case.

I was seeing a psychiatrist at the time to help me adjust to the service. He was very nice, and I liked him a lot. I talked to him about her, told him I was so miserable I couldn't sleep at night. He put me on 100 mg of Benadryl, but my situation only seemed to get worse.

One day, I took the bottle of Benadryl to my next-door neighbor and asked her if she would keep it for me. I just wanted to get it out of my house. I was suffering from insomnia and depression. I guess she called Captain Alfred and told him what happened. To make a long story short, they put me in a small room in the hospital and kept me there for several days.

They eventually transferred me to the ward, Major C's ward, and she would come in every day and order me around—make my bed, do this, do that. I told my doctor about it. He got a stern look on his face and marched himself right down to her desk. I could hear him all the way down the hall. He told her to leave me alone, that I was a patient and was sick. He went on and on. She never bothered me again.

After some time passed, I got out of the hospital and had some time off. I had an appointment with Captain Alfred, and he showed me a letter Major C had written to our CO. She had lied about things I'd supposedly done and was trying to get me kicked out of the service. Captain Alfred made me an appointment with the CO.

Later on, I went to see the CO. He was so nice, like a father figure. We talked for quite a while. He told me not to worry, I hadn't done anything to warrant a discharge. I did some hard thinking, figured I'd probably have to work with Major C again, and decided I just couldn't take that chance. So, I took an honorable discharge and went back to Oklahoma.

My Marriage

I had a very unhappy marriage, though I was crazy about my husband, Jan. The first year was good, but after that it went downhill. He said I snored, so he slept in the spare room, but he was a womanizer, and at night, when I was asleep, he would sneak out and go cat around. I didn't like it, but I didn't feel like I could do much about it.

We would go out to eat every night, which makes for a poor diet. I was eating all the wrong things. This went on for ages. I kept gaining weight, but I was so depressed I didn't care. I gained about 225 pounds. I spent a lot of time crying in those days.

Jan was a welder and was good at it. He made good money and liked it a lot. I can't remember what happened, but welders were out and so Jan lost his job. This lasted for years. He wouldn't even look for a job. I was on his back about it all the time, and we bickered about it to no avail. Believe it or not, I actually married the man twice! We did have some good times, but the bad always seemed to outweigh the good.

I was eventually diagnosed with manic depression. I was depressed most of the time and was in and out of the Oklahoma VA Psychiatric Unit. I would get well and go home, but it was no time till I had to go back to the hospital again. This went on for years. I was also diagnosed with diabetes, neuropathy, thyroid trouble, irritable bowel syndrome, and high blood pressure.

In 1967, after I returned home from having Alan, my first child, Jan and I were in a bad car accident. We didn't have seat belts back then. I lost eight teeth when I hit the dashboard and broke my ankle when I hit the floorboard. Jan lost four teeth on the steering wheel and had a concussion. We were so lucky the baby wasn't with us at the time. Before we left the house, an elderly neighbor came by and offered to watch Alan while Jan took me to work. God was in control, no telling what the baby's fate would have been otherwise, if he had been with us.

Jan's aunt, from Texas, came and got Alan while we were in the hospital. I was in the hospital for a week or two and Jan was there for five days. He signed out against medical advice so he could go see Alan. It was a horrid experience.

I worked as a head charge nurse at St. Anthony Hospital. I loved it. I worked there for seven years. I worked at several different places, but Deaconess Hospital was my favorite place. I divorced Jan around that time but took him back later that year. I worked at Deaconess for about three years but was asked to leave because of my manic depression. It just about killed me to have to leave Deaconess. I worked other jobs, but my heart wasn't in it. Eventually my disease got the best of me, and I couldn't function as a nurse. It broke my heart, because I loved being a nurse so much.

Jan and I separated five or six times. He would always get into trouble when he was away from me! He went to prison three times. The first time, the charge was armed robbery. The second time, I can't remember. And the third time was for bank robbery.

The first time he was in, I rode with a friend, each of us visiting our husbands every weekend. After Jan robbed the bank he sat down on the curb with the money. He told the police that it was getting cold, and he needed the money to put a roof over his head. I had moved to Wisconsin, but my friends in Oklahoma saw it on TV. Jan wrote me often over the years.

When Jan got out of prison, he was diagnosed with an abdominal aneurysm. The VA hospital doctors wanted to operate on him, but he refused because they told him he might be paralyzed. He rented a small apartment. He would walk to Walmart (it was a long way), and he was having a lot of pain. He lived a quiet life and did the best he could with his health issues.

We had a mutual friend, and he would go use her phone to call me. This went on for some time, until he ruptured his aneurysm.

They rushed Jan by ambulance to the Midwest City Memorial Hospital. The hospital contacted me, to get permission to operate, which I did. The nurse, who talked to me, said he only had a three percent chance of making it. Well, he survived but was paralyzed from the waist down and placed on a respirator.

I would call him, but, of course, he couldn't talk. I would hear him mumble, though, so I knew he could hear me and was trying to talk to me. As time went on, he developed complications. He had tubes in his stomach, because of an infection they couldn't get rid of, which drained into a bag on the floor. He had to have a tracheotomy.

They kept him for a long time. I felt they were experimenting on him because he didn't have insurance. Eventually, they sent him to the Oklahoma VA Hospital in Oklahoma City.

I was concerned about Jan's salvation and talked to my pastor about him. My pastor told me to contact my old pastor in Oklahoma and ask him to pay Jan a visit. The pastor was out of town for the weekend, but he eventually called me back and said he would be glad to go see Jan. He called me sometime later and told me that Jan had accepted the Lord. So, I didn't have to worry anymore, he would be in Heaven waiting for me some day.

I talked to the nurses to see if I could try to talk to him like I had before. The nurse said he didn't want to talk to me, which blew me away.

The doctor, who was the director of the ICU, called me and asked me if I knew what Jan's wishes were concerning his life. I told him that he refused the surgery at the other hospital because he might be paralyzed. I knew in my heart that his quality of life was so poor and that there was no hope of getting better. The doctor thanked me for talking to him and said they would pull the plug on the respirator. He gave me the date and time this would occur. Now that I was assured of Jan's salvation, I felt better knowing his fate. The doctor mentioned to me that they would see to it that he was asleep so he could be comfortable. My husband passed away from that ruptured abdominal aneurysm.

I finally went on welfare; my kids had to eat. I was keeping my elderly mother and my two children. I didn't get a welfare check for three months. One day the apartment manager and her associate came to see me. They said I was a good tenant, but they had to have my back rent in a week, otherwise we would have to leave. I cried and cried all night. My son, Alan, who was about eight years old at the time, stayed outside my room all night long. The next day I went to check my mail and there was a check from the Veterans Administration for $5,000.

That was a godsend. I paid off my rent and my bills. I was a happy camper. I am now a one hundred percent service-connected vet.

Weight Loss

Back in 2002, I started getting serious about my weight problem. I had gone to Weight Watchers many times in the past. I'd get off forty pounds and gain it back in a year, but this time I made up my mind I was going to take it off for good. I practiced portion control, drank lots of fluids, and got lots of exercise. It took me a year to get it off, but, with God's help, I did it.

There were ups and downs, of course. At one point I gained back thirty pounds, but I got that off, too. I got down to 122 pounds. That's the smallest I've ever been. I make a game of it, and it works every time. I got into water aerobics three times a week. I exercised with weights for my triceps, and I worked on my stomach, too. I have a picture of myself from before the weight loss, and no one recognizes me.

My dramatic weight loss did wonders for me—no more oxygen, no inhaler, no nebulizer, no more insulin or any diabetic medicine. Best of all, I'm free from diabetes. I weigh myself once a week, on Tuesday, and if I ever go over 125 pounds, I alter my diet. I would have a light breakfast; a twelve-gram protein bar and a hundred calories of light popcorn for lunch; and then for dinner, a salad, hot vegetable, and either fish or chicken. Works every time to lose weight.

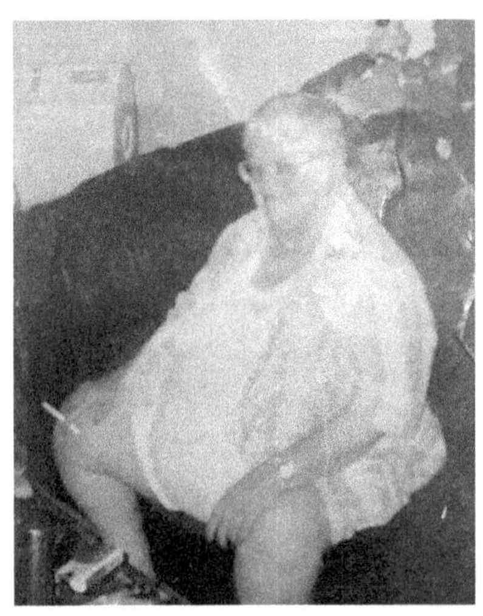

My Health

I was sick off and on for two years, during 2002-2004. I was in the hospital three times, and in and out of the VA ER several times. I was diagnosed with aspiration pneumonia. When I was in the VA ICU, I arrested, and they brought me back. The doctors told my daughter, Janine, they didn't know what kind of brain function I would have. I was there a week and a half. The doctors told Janine they wouldn't release me unless I had someone with me 24/7, so she became my nurse. I had rubbed a large black blister on my ankle. I had to return on an outpatient basis frequently. It took eight months to heal.

They taught Janine how to care for it. I had to have oxygen at night. I had to use a walker and an elevated shoe. It was miserable. Later on that year, I had to be hospitalized with the flu and pneumonia, too. I was having a lot of trouble breathing. I went to the ER and they checked out my heart.

My Daughter

My daughter, Janine, was very special to me. She lived with me for five years, from 2002-2005. She cooked for me and never used a recipe, and it always turned out great. She was an excellent housekeeper.

For the last two years of that time, I felt pretty puny. One time, I had a bladder infection and they put me on sulfa. I was so sick. I fell ten times in one day. Janine put me in a wheelchair and told me not to get up. She took me off my sulfa, and the next day I was fine. They put me on another medicine after that, and it worked well.

I couldn't drive anymore so Janine would take me on drives, and if she ever saw anyone who looked like they needed help, she would pull over to the side of the road and give them money. She was tender-hearted and enjoyed helping people. She also took me to the VA for my appointments since I wasn't up to riding with RSVP (a Rides for Veterans program) at the time.

She would come into my room at bedtime and check my oxygen. Then she would have me crawl over to the middle of the bed, so that if I rolled over, I wouldn't be too close to the edge. She would even bring me ice water to drink during the night. Sometimes we would have words, but we always made up before we slept. When she tucked me in, she would give me a kiss and a hug, and tell me how much she loved me. I think that is my fondest memory of her. It brings tears to my eyes. I miss her so.

She had a wonderful sense of humor. She had a great wit and had lots of funny stories she would tell me. And since she was a hairdresser, she would always cut my hair, and it would always please me. She even cut my toenails for me.

My daughter passed away on March 6, 2018. The police told me that she was found in her bed, deceased. It was unexpected, so, of course, there was no easy way to break it to me. They asked if I wanted to talk to the police chaplain. I said yes, and he came and spoke about his condolences and wanted to know if he could notify someone for me. So, I asked him to call my pastor and his wife. They arrived within fifteen minutes. They were such a comfort to me. They called my granddaughter's adopted mother to have her bring my granddaughter, Brie, to me. It was the hardest thing I had to do, to tell her about her mom. I had been crying a lot, but knew I had to be strong for her. I tried to be as gentle as I could. She was devastated, but she had to know about it. Our pastor and his wife stayed a long time, so, somehow, we got threw it.

I called the VA hospital and told them I had just lost my daughter and was having a hard time and needed help. I had an appointment set up within two hours. I saw a social worker and my psychiatrist. They were so very kind and helpful. I'm bipolar, which was why I needed to call them.

I don't know how I would have gotten through it if it hadn't been for my pastor, his wife, and my church family. We had a wonderful memorial service, which was very nice. My granddaughter, my grandson, and I all had a part in the eulogy. It was so sweet and well attended. Thirty members of my church were there, even though my daughter had only visited the church once or twice. I made it through a very difficult time because of all the support from my church.

My Granddaughter

Now my favorite subject: my granddaughter, Brie. I kept her for six months when she was five years old, while her mom was away. We had a great time. She was so feisty, and I had to do my best to keep up with her. I lost fifteen  pounds during that time! She told me once that that was the best time of her life.

At the time of this writing, she is seventeen, and a junior in high school. She is a cheerleader and works three days a week at a restaurant. She has to attend all the sports activities at the school.

She makes good grades and plans to go to college at the University of Wisconsin. She wants to be a nurse like her grandmother, then wants to become a midwife. She hopes for a scholarship and will apply for grants that she doesn't have to pay back. She has a job as a nanny this summer for two children, ages seven and nine. The pay is very good! She takes college-level Spanish, which she's had four years of. I think that will help her with future jobs.

I don't get to see her very often, since she's so busy with her activities. She plans to spend three whole days with me during spring break. I sure look forward to that. I know we will both see her mom and oldest sister in Heaven someday. Her sister passed away with leukemia, when she was only four years old.

My Son

My son, Alan, was a big part of my life. I really enjoyed life with my son.

His wrestling coach in college called me one day and told me that Alan had been named Athlete of the Year and that we were invited to the awards ceremony. The whole thing was a big surprise. We didn't end up going, though, because my husband said it was too far to drive. I was so mad at him. They said he won the award because he went to wrestling practice every day at six in the morning, worked a full-time job, was married, and had a straight-A average. At the end of the year he was good enough to go to something like the world series of wrestling (it wasn't called that, but you know what I mean). He was twenty-five years old, and he was wrestling eighteen-year-old boys in their prime. He didn't place, but I believe he was in the top ten. He had been wrestling since he was nine years old, for the YMCA, then continued it through junior high and high school. I was so proud of him.

When I lived in Oklahoma, he always sent me a dozen long-stemmed red roses for my birthday and Mother's Day.

I once flew to Amsterdam to visit him and his wife. He was stationed in Germany in the Army. We had a wonderful time.

The three of us took a train to Paris. His wife had a map, so with her as the navigator, we walked all over Paris. It was a blast. We saw all the sights. We were worn out by the end of it. We were so tired that night that we slept in our clothes. We had breakfast at a quaint little restaurant the next morning.

I spent three weeks with them. One day, I decided to take a walk. The streets there didn't seem all that different from the streets back home. I turned the corner and walked and walked, but never found another street to get me home, so I turned around and went back the way I came. I came across a grocery store. There was no front to it. I saw a little old woman with her little dog. Just guess what the dog had in its mouth—a head of lettuce! I wanted to laugh but didn't want to hurt her feelings.

We were running late the next day to catch the train and we missed it. My son was upset because he was taking a class in college and had a big test. Luckily, his professor let him reschedule. I will never forget that wonderful trip.

My son and I were so close, and then, all of a sudden, my world fell apart. He stopped coming around, didn't call anymore. I did everything in my power to contact him, but to no avail. We hadn't had words or anything. As I write this, that would have been nine years ago. I was devastated and heartbroken. I used to cry every Mother's Day. I did this for a long time, but finally I stopped crying and started praying for him! I know it is in God's hands, and I feel that someday he will return to me. I know he loves me as I do him, and time will tell.

I asked my daughter once to take me to see if we could find his new house, because I knew he had moved. I was going to give him a card, to let him know that I was thinking of him. We went by his house, or what used to be his house, and my daughter said she saw him and his girl outside, looking at the siding. She pulled around the corner and I took the card up to the door. He had some steep stairs, and I fell and screamed. My daughter came running, she heard me from around the block. I thought he should have heard me, too, but he didn't come out. It made me sad. He just must have issues. I took the card and put it in his mailbox.

Another time, Janine told me she ran into him at a convenience store. She called his name, and he turned around and came over to her. He hugged her and told her how good she looked. She said to him, "Why don't you call Mom, she misses you so much." He said, "I don't want to." Then he just walked away. I spent years and lots of effort trying to contact him. Eventually, I decided to just let it go.

After my daughter passed, my granddaughter went to his house. He didn't recognize her, of course. It had been nine years since he last saw her, after all. She told him about her mom, and he was very upset. She gave him my telephone number and left, but I haven't heard from him.

My Church

One of my favorite places to be is in church. I look forward to Sundays so that I can go to church with my church family. We have services three times a week—Sunday School and the Sunday morning service, Sunday evening, and Wednesday evening. On Wednesday, we also have a prayer service, where they hand out paper for prayer requests. People ask for prayers for needy people, and then we all take the paper home and say prayers for everyone on the list every day of the week. We have an outstanding pastor, and he and his wife are both terrific leaders of our church. God is the center of my life.

The Brewers

My favorite pastime is Milwaukee Brewer baseball. I never miss a game. I talk to each batter, the pitcher, the coach, and sometimes the umpires. I even dream about the Brewers.

I remember when they beat the Cubs in the playoffs, winning the division championship. They had won twelve games in a row, before the playoffs. They did great, and I was so proud of them for all their effort. I am a die-hard baseball fan.

It's always a long winter without the games, but then they go into spring training, and I get to watch some games. Then comes April, and look out, they start their season. My daughter once told me that she couldn't believe I watched the pre-games, the games, *and* the post games.

My Life Now

As I write this, I weigh 122 pounds. I have lost a 102 pounds. This is the happiest and most fulfilled I have ever been. I have high aspirations for my future. I'm a retired nurse and a former lieutenant in the USAF. I have never been so healthy. I keep a positive attitude and rarely have a bad day. I attribute my wonderful life to the good Lord.

God is in control of my life and always has been. Some people might say my life was tragic, but I have learned to roll with the punches and to just keep on truckin'. I can hardly wait for the next day to come so I can see what joy it brings me.

My church family is the best of the best. They keep me going. On Wednesday nights, you'll see me in prayer meeting. My whole church is praying for my son's salvation, and has been for several years. It's been nine years since he left me, but I know in my heart that someday, when I least expect it, he will return to my life, and I will praise the Lord.

I have never been in better shape physically, mentally, socially, or financially. You just can't get much better than that. I go to the Senior Center, when I have some spare time. They are so nice to you there. A transit bus  comes to your door and picks you up and takes you home for a dollar. For two dollars, they take me to Skaalan, a local nursing and rehabilitation center, three times a week for my water aerobics. They'll take you to different places to shop, too, even the malls in Madison on Fridays.

I have a wonderful case manager who is so much fun and full of life. And pretty, too. She is helping me with my book. I know that it might not ever get published, but you don't know until you try. It is great fun to dream. I am joining a writer's group at the Senior Center. I'm so excited about it all. We checked for information on hiring a ghostwriter, but it costs $1,900, so we consider that a last resort.

I have a good friend from my church, she considers me her ministry. I don't drive anymore, and I turned my car into the dealer for a voluntary repo. They fixed it up and sold it for $10,000. All I had to pay them was $685, which beats me paying off the $10,000. Anyway, my friend drives all over the place and I give her a $50 gift certificate every so often. I don't know what I would do without her.

The rest of the time the senior transit takes me where I need to go for two bucks. I have only used the taxi once, so I have been blessed and very fortunate. I still have my driver's license, and plan to keep it up. Maybe someday I'll want to drive again.

The Retreat

On April 5 and 6, 2019, seven of us ladies from church went to Green Lakes, Wisconsin, for a retreat. The pastor's wife drove us there in the church van, and we stayed overnight at a fancy motel. The weather was warm. There were 560 women that were registered. They were from Baptist churches from all over Wisconsin. This was the largest retreat I have ever been to.

The lake there was the deepest in the state and the grounds were mammoth. It was like a huge campus, with many huge buildings. We walked everywhere. I had never been there before, but several members of our group had. If not for them, I would have been lost.

On Friday, we had lunch, then a Singspiration in Pillsbury Hall. Then we heard the main speaker, followed by two workshops. They had to split us up so they could seat us all, there were so many women. After dinner, we had another Singspiration and a general session with the main speaker. They had wonderful speakers for all the workshops, as well as the main speaker.

On Saturday, we had a breakfast buffet, then two more workshops. After lunch, we returned to Pillsbury Hall for another stirring Singspiration session. One song we sang talked about the Lord coming to see us, and I was so moved I got choked up and couldn't  continue to sing. I had cold chills running up and down my legs. That was a God moment, for sure. I could feel His presence. Then we heard the main speaker again and had a safe trip home.

During this retreat, I had a private room. I hoped I would sleep better, being by myself, but it didn't work out that way. I only slept two or three hours the whole night. It has been my experience, when I went to other retreats and didn't sleep well, that I would be in really bad shape and would feel terrible the next day. And then, despite the fact that I enjoyed it, by the time I got home, I'd feel sick. So, I figured it would be the same way as it had been in the past, but God must have had his hand on me, because I never ever got sleepy or sick. It was just a miracle, which sure humbled me. I can only say God was in control through the whole thing and I greatly appreciated it. Praise the Lord!

My Routine

My daily routine keeps me going. I get up at 6:30 AM, take my shower, and eat breakfast. I ride my recumbent bike for almost an hour. I have my daily devotions for an hour or two. In the afternoon, some more devotions, read from "Our Daily Bread" and from "Faith to Faith," a daily guide to victory. I also read a book called "God Hears Her." It is written for women, by women, and has 365 answers to what Jesus would do. On Monday and Thursday, I go for lunch at the Senior Center. On Tuesday and Friday, I go to the wellness center at Skaalen for water aerobics. Wednesday is church night, with the prayer meeting. After lunch I take a twenty-minute power nap and then do my exercises for my tummy and two different ones using weights. I never get bored. I don't have time to!

Camp American Legion

Once a year, I spend a week's vacation at Camp American Legion in June. Wisconsin veteran women get together from all over the  state and have the time of their lives. This year will be the fourth year in a row that I go. The camp is located three or four hours up north. It's picturesque, built around Lake Tomahawk. It is just so beautiful up there. I can see why they call it God's Country.

Everything is free, as far as food and lodging. The only thing that you are responsible for is transportation to and from camp. Different places provide buses to and from. They provide canoes and pontoon boats for fishing. They'll even bait your hook for you if you are squeamish. They have workshops. We took a pontoon boat trip to Minocqua where we went shopping and out to lunch with our friends. It was so much fun.

The food is fantastic, and there's a lot of it. There are fourteen cabins, all quaint and cozy. They have a sweet chapel for us, and we all enjoy it so much. They have a beautiful lodge where we eat, and it's really nice. They have rooms upstairs for people that need private rooms. Last year I had a semi-private room with a TV, fridge, and shower.

They treat you like queens there. The American Legion Auxiliary brings everybody presents, and different groups of volunteers bring us things, too. Once you go to Camp American Legion, you can't wait to go back. Everyone is so friendly. The workers up there are all volunteers. The director and his whole family work there. I heard from a fellow camper that they are already accepting applications for next year. You see a lot of familiar faces, of the people coming back. I can't wait to go back myself come June.

My Faith

I often talk to the Lord's picture, high up on my wall, above all my other pictures. I talk to Him about what I'm putting in my book, and then I think that I should put *that* in my book. I feel God inspires me with thoughts. I feel the Lord is helping me to write my book, because I look to Him for guidance.

I have had some very difficult times in my life, when I was in the deepest despair. In those times, I thought God had forgotten me, but He was always there. It sometimes felt like my prayers never left my room. I got away from church for months and months. I even thought

my church had forgotten me. And the more
church I missed, the worse I felt. I took my eyes
off of Jesus, but He never took his eyes off of
me. I can think back over my life and see how
He brought me through, each and every time. I
finally learned to roll with the punches, and if I
ever run out of rope, to tie a knot and bounce
back. I know now that God is always in control.
I now have Jesus in my heart, soul, and mind.
By His grace, I have found a wonderful peace
that I have never known.

THE END

To hear Bonnie's oral history that was recorded for the Wisconsin Veterans Museum on November 19, 2018, scan the QR code below: